CLIMATE CHANGE
iN TEMPERATE ZONES

STUART BAKER

Marshall Cavendish
Benchmark

New York

This edition first published in 2010 in the United States of America
by Marshall Cavendish Benchmark.

Marshall Cavendish Benchmark
99 White Plains Road
Tarrytown, NY 10591
www.marshallcavendish.us

First published in 2009 by
MACMILLAN EDUCATION AUSTRALIA PTY LTD
15–19 Claremont Street, South Yarra 3141

Visit our website at www.macmillan.com.au or go directly to www.macmillanlibrary.com.au

Associated companies and representatives throughout the world.

Library of Congress Cataloging-in-Publication Data

Baker, Stuart
    In temperate zones / by Stuart Baker.
        p. cm. – (Climate change)
    Includes index.
    ISBN 978-0-7614-4441-1
    1. Climatic changes–Juvenile literature. 2. Climatic changes–Environmental aspects–Juvenile
literature. 3. Temperate climate–Juvenile literature. I. Title.
    QC981.8.C5B355 2009
    551.6912–dc22
                                    2009005769

Edited by Sally Woollett
Text and cover design by Christine Deering
Page layout by Christine Deering
Illustrations by Richard Morden
Photo research by Legend Images

Printed in the United States

Acknowledgments
The author and the publisher are grateful to the following for permission to reproduce
copyright material:

Front cover photograph: Bushfire courtesy of Photolibrary/IFA-BILDERTEAM GMBH
Photos courtesy of:
CO2CRC - Cooperative Research Centre for Greenhouse Gas Technologies, **29** (top); ©
Enjoylife25/Dreamstime.com, **10**; © Rybina/Dreamstime.com, **26**; Ali Burafi/AFP/Getty Images,
23; Peter Parks/AFP/Getty Images, **22**; Nigel Cattlin/Getty Images, **21**; © John Armstrong-Millar/
iStockphoto, **9**; © Grant Dougall/iStockphoto, **29** (bottom); © LyaC/iStockphoto, **19**; © Wendy
Rentz/iStockphoto, **14**; © Scott Vickers/iStockphoto, **24**; © Newspix/News Ltd/Frank Violi, **17**;
Photolibrary/Lanz Von Horsten/ABPL, **15**; Photolibrary © Ashley Cooper/Alamy, **30**; Photolibrary/
IFA-BILDERTEAM GMBH, **25**; Photolibrary/Peter Weimann, **13**; © Dean Mitchell/Shutterstock, **11**;
© Emily Veinglory/Shutterstock, **20**; Heinz Slupetzky, Salzburg, **12** (left); Wikimedia Commons,
photo by Otberg, **12** (right)

1 3 5 6 4 2

Contents

Glossary Words	When a word is printed in **bold**, you can look up its meaning in the Glossary on page 31.

Climate Change

Earth has been warming and cooling for millions of years. During the **Ice Age**, large areas of Europe and Canada were covered with **glaciers**. Earth's climate was 5.4–9°Fahrenheit (3–5°Celsius) cooler than it is today. The most recent Ice Age ended 20,000 years ago.

Fact ZONE
Today, Earth's average surface temperature is 59°F (15°C).

Rising Temperatures

Temperatures across the world are rising at a rate faster than ever before. Earth's average temperature has risen by 1.08°F (0.6°C) in the past one hundred years. The ten hottest years on record occurred over the past fourteen years. The hottest year ever recorded was 2005. This **global warming** may be enough to cause changes in weather patterns, which is commonly referred to as **climate change**.

Earth's Climate Zones

Earth can be divided into four main types of climate zones:

- Arctic
- Temperate
- Tropical
- Antarctic

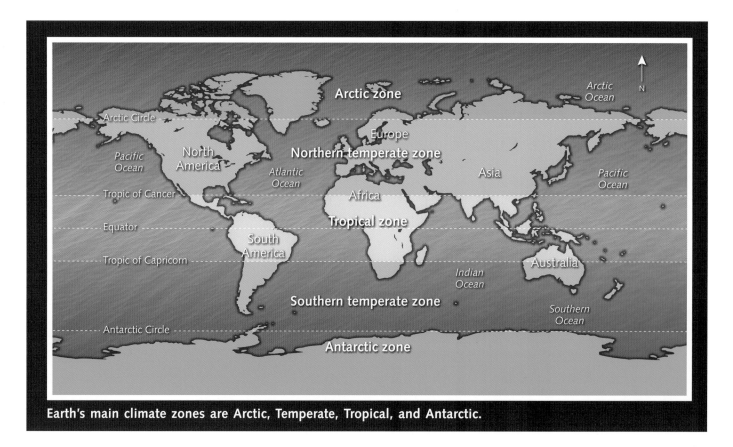

Earth's main climate zones are Arctic, Temperate, Tropical, and Antarctic.

The Temperate Region

The Earth has two temperate zones. They are located in the mid-**latitudes** on either side of the **equator**. The northern temperate zone extends from the Tropic of Cancer to the Arctic Circle. The southern temperate zone extends from the Tropic of Capricorn to the Antarctic Circle. Europe and large parts of the Americas, Australia, southern Africa, and Russia lie within the temperate zones.

Favorable Climate

The temperate zones have moderate conditions, not the extremes of temperature found in other parts of the world. Most places in the temperate zones have four seasons each year. The temperate zones are some of the most productive farming areas on Earth with a favorable climate and rich soil. Over hundreds of years of human occupation, the land has been cleared for farming though a few of the original forests still remain.

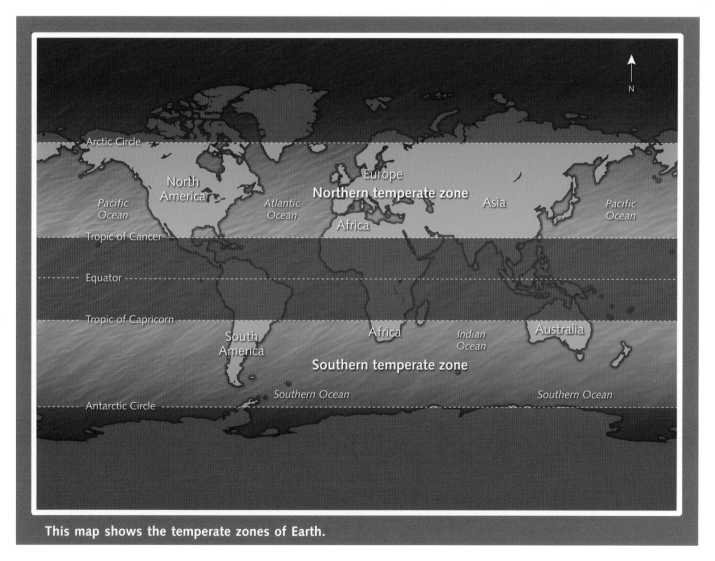

This map shows the temperate zones of Earth.

Global Warming and Greenhouse Gases

Global warming is caused by the **greenhouse effect. Greenhouse gases** trap the heat from the sun in Earth's **atmosphere**. This heat leads to an increase in Earth's surface temperature.

Greenhouse Gases

Greenhouse gases occur naturally in Earth's atmosphere, but human activities contribute to these gases. These human activities are increasing as the world's population increases.

Scientists now agree that in recent decades the amount of greenhouse gases in the atmosphere has increased. More of the sun's heat is being trapped, leading to further global warming. The term "global warming" in this book refers to the effects of this extra heat being trapped.

The Impact of Human Activities

Human activities generate three main greenhouse gases: **carbon dioxide**, **methane**, and **nitrous oxide**. Carbon dioxide is produced when **fossil fuels** such as coal and oil are burned. The level of carbon dioxide in the air is also affected by the clearing of forests, as trees and other plants absorb carbon dioxide to produce oxygen, which is vital to life on Earth. Methane is produced naturally by livestock such as cows and sheep who release it as part of their digestive process. It is also produced when substances such as manure and waste products in landfills begin to ferment, or turn sour. Nitrous oxide is produced when certain fertilizers are used to grow crops.

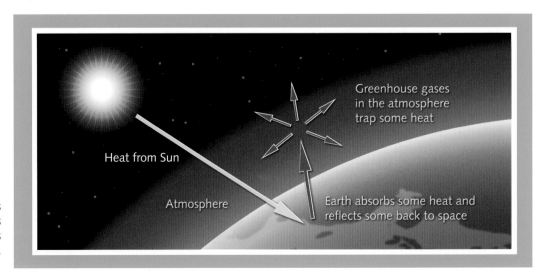

Heat from Sun

Greenhouse gases in the atmosphere trap some heat

Atmosphere

Earth absorbs some heat and reflects some back to space

The greenhouse effect is the trapping of the Sun's heat due to certain gases in the atmosphere.

Possible Effects of Global Warming

Scientists are making predictions about the effects of global warming. Global warming could affect the environment and humans in many different ways.

Fact ZONE

Rising temperatures have caused most of Earth's mass **extinction** events.

POSSIBLE EFFECTS OF GLOBAL WARMING IN THE TEMPERATE ZONES

POSSIBLE EVENT	PREDICTED RESULT	IMPACT IN TEMPERATE ZONES
MELTING OF ICE	✳ **Retreating** mountain **glaciers** ✳ Milder and shorter winters	✳ Closing of ski resorts on lower slopes due to lack of snow
WARM AND MOIST CONDITIONS	✳ Air pollution	✳ More breathing problems
EXTREME WEATHER CONDITIONS AND MORE EL NIÑO AND LA NIÑA EVENTS	✳ Greater frequency and intensity of flooding, drought and record-breaking temperatures	✳ Heat-related illness and death ✳ Low fish catches in the Pacific Ocean ✳ Threats to property and life by fire ✳ Spreading of disease during floods ✳ Lower crop yields for farmers in southern Australia and in the wheat belts of the United States
REDUCING **ALPINE ZONES**	✳ Changing **habitat** range for animal and plant species	✳ Adjustment for some species and extinction of others ✳ Loss of **biodiversity** ✳ Some earlier breeding seasons

Climate Change in Temperate Zones

Countries in the temperate zones are experiencing a range of climatic changes. In some areas, warmer temperatures have meant more frequent heatwaves and drought conditions. Other areas have received more rainfall.

Temperatures are expected to increase a further 3.6–11.3°F (2–6.3°C) in Europe in the next one hundred years. Environment experts in Europe believe that within fifty years Europeans will experience new and possibly hazardous conditions. According to recent reports, extreme weather events will probably become more frequent.

Similar extreme conditions are being felt in Australia where rainfall patterns are changing. Northwestern Australia is expected to receive more rainfall in the future while the east and southwest regions are expected to experience less rainfall.

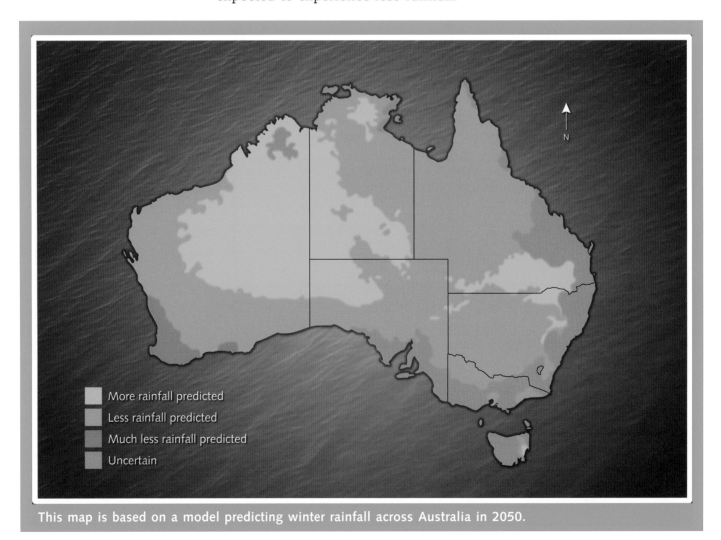

More rainfall predicted
Less rainfall predicted
Much less rainfall predicted
Uncertain

This map is based on a model predicting winter rainfall across Australia in 2050.

Heatwaves and Droughts

Southern Europe will have longer and more severe heatwaves and droughts. This will put strain on water supplies and increase the risk of forest fires in countries around the Mediterranean Sea. In 2003, the Po River in Italy was at its lowest levels in one hundred years.

Winters will be milder and shorter, which will shorten the winter sports season in the Alps and reduce the season's snowfall.

Flooding

Higher rainfall is predicted over most of Europe in the winter. More frequent flooding could destroy crops and livestock and disrupt transportation and communications. Property destruction will result in huge damage bills and raise insurance costs.

High temperatures mean warmer air, which can hold more moisture. This means that, even in a dry summer, rainfall could be much heavier.

Changing Alpine Zones

Alpine zones are becoming smaller because temperatures are rising higher up the mountains. Some animal and plant species can adjust to some temperature change, but others may die out.

Fact ZONE

During the 2003 heatwave in Paris temperatures were higher than 104°F (40°C) and caused the deaths of about 20,000 people.

Fact ZONE

In August 2002 major floods over parts of central Europe left the historic cities of Dresden, Germany, and Prague, Czech Republic, flooded, and more than one hundred people drowned.

This river flooded parts of southern France in 2006.

The Natural World of Temperate Zones

Temperate zones support a variety of large and small mammals living in the forests and grassy plains. In the alpine zone of the mountains trees are replaced by alpine meadows.

Deciduous Forests

Deciduous forests, which shed their leaves in the fall, were the original tree cover of the temperate zones. Although they have been cleared for cities and farms over the years, some large forested areas still remain. These can be found in North America, Europe, Japan, and New Zealand. Within the forests trees such as ash, oak, beech, chestnut, and elm change in four distinct seasons. In the fall the leaves change brilliant colors of red and gold. In the winter the trees go into an inactive state and lose them. As the warmer months of spring approach new leaves appear.

Deciduous trees change their leaf color and shed them in the fall.

The Deciduous Forest Ecosystem

The deciduous forest **ecosystem** supports mammals such as deer, brown bears, beavers, and red squirrels, and insects such as beetles. Most of the animals are nut and acorn feeders or they eat plants and other animals.

Grasslands

The grasslands in North America, called prairies, and those of Asia, known as steppe, provide food for a number of large animal species.

Red squirrels collect nuts in the fall months and hibernate during the winter.

Alpine Zones

Background

Alpine zones occur in the mountainous regions of the temperate zones. In these areas snow and ice build up on the mountain peaks. The Himalayan alpine zone contains about 15,000 glaciers. The water produced when they melt flows into nine major river systems which support 1.3 billion people downstream in India, China, and Bangladesh.

Alpine zones support a wide variety of plants and animals.

As mountain areas become warmer, glaciers are retreating. Animals and plants are moving up the mountains to areas that were once too cold for them.

The shrinking of the Pasterze glacier, in Austria, can be seen by comparing it in 1875 (left) and 2005 (right).

Glaciers in Retreat

Glaciers are slow-moving frozen rivers that develop due to the build-up of ice in mountainous regions. Glaciers are in retreat in the Himalayas, Rockies, Andes, Alps, and in the mountains of New Zealand. Two-thirds of China's Himalayan glaciers are likely to disappear by 2050.

CASE STUDY

Populating Pine Beetles

Pine beetles bore into the bark of trees to lay their eggs, eventually killing the tree. Pine beetles are killed by frost and in most years their numbers have been controlled. However, recent mild winters have resulted in a massive increase in the number of pine beetles. In British Columbia, Canada, pine beetles may kill three-quarters of the pine forest by 2015.

Pine beetles are destroying this forest in Glacier National Park in the United States.

Loss of Habitat and Diversity

Global warming is reducing alpine zones because temperatures are rising higher up the mountains. If the alpine zone disappears, plant and animal species that cannot adjust to the higher temperatures will die out. This would be a great loss of biodiversity.

Fact ZONE

The red squirrel of North America may benefit from global warming. Female red squirrels are giving birth eighteen days earlier in the season than their grandmothers, so their babies are more independent when it is time to store food in the fall. As a result, more squirrels are surviving the winter.

Birds

Background

Many species of birds are found in the temperate zones. They include finches, sparrows, thrushes, and larger birds of prey such as hawks and eagles. Many **migrate** to warmer regions in the winter, although some can survive the colder months.

Warmer temperatures of the spring are arriving earlier in many parts of temperate zones. Some bird species may be able to respond better to this change than others.

Robins in the United Kingdom are laying their eggs earlier because of climate change.

Early Egg-Laying

In response to early spring warmth one-third of the sixty bird species studied in the United Kingdom are laying their eggs more than one week earlier in the season than they did fifteen years ago. This is a problem if chicks are hatching before food such as insects, is available.

Changed Migration Patterns

As temperatures become higher some migratory birds such as the pied flycatcher are arriving at their breeding grounds earlier in the season. The timing of the arrival at the breeding ground is important because enough food has to be available for the young birds.

Extreme weather events may affect the ability of some birds to complete their migration.

CASE STUDY

Double Breeding Season for Owls

Higher temperatures in Europe in 2002 resulted in an explosion in the mice, vole, and rat population. Tawny and barn owls feed on these animals. With such an abundant food supply they nested early and produced chicks twice in one year.

Higher temperatures make more food for rats, which means more food for owls.

El Niño and La Niña

Background

El Niño (el *neen* yo) is a Spanish word meaning "christ child" or "boy child."

La Niña (la *neen* ya) means "girl child."

These terms are used to describe a pattern of ocean currents that happens every few years in the Pacific Ocean near South America.

Fact ZONE

The term El Niño was first used by fishermen from Peru in South America, who noticed that a warm ocean current affected their Pacific Ocean fishing grounds.

During an El Niño or La Niña event, changes in the wind and ocean currents take place that affect climate patterns across the world. As greenhouse gases build up in the atmosphere we can expect more extreme El Niño events such as floods and fires.

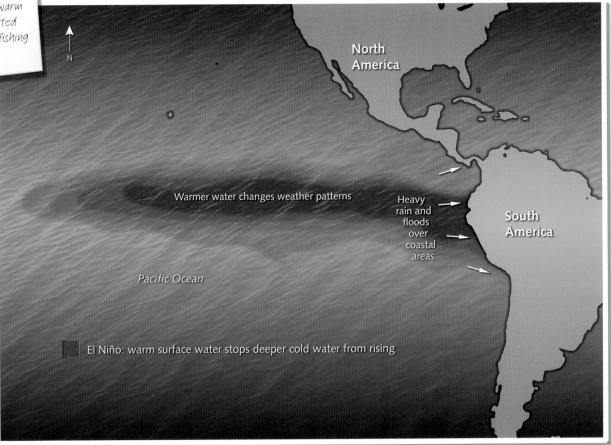

North America

Warmer water changes weather patterns

Heavy rain and floods over coastal areas

South America

Pacific Ocean

El Niño: warm surface water stops deeper cold water from rising

An El Niño event changes Pacific Ocean currents.

Less Food for Fish

In most years the cold water from the deeper ocean is drawn to the surface off the coast of Peru. When El Niño occurs, this upwelling of cold water, which contains the small animals that fish such as anchovies eat, is blocked by the warm surface water, resulting in less food for the anchovies.

Floods and Droughts

Warmer water over the eastern Pacific Ocean results in floods and very heavy rain over the South American coast. In the western Pacific cooler water upwells, producing droughts in Australia, Indonesia and South Africa.

During a La Niña event winds blow westward across the Pacific Ocean, pushing the warm surface water toward Australia. This results in higher than normal rainfall and flooding.

CASE STUDY

Droughts in Australia, 1983

During the 1982 El Niño event some of the lowest recorded winter and spring rainfalls occurred in southeastern Australia. Large areas were affected by drought. On February 16, 1983, fires broke out in Victoria and South Australia due to dry, hot, and windy conditions. They were one of the deadliest fires ever recorded. Apart from the tragic loss of human life, thousands of livestock were destroyed.

The 1982–1983 drought affected many parts of Australia, including Bourke in New South Wales.

Humans in Temperate Zones

Temperate zones include most of the world's developed countries including the United States, Japan, the United Kingdom, Germany, and Australia. Not all countries of the temperate zones are wealthy, such as Afghanistan, one of the world's ten poorest countries.

In Europe, North America, Australia, and parts of Asia most people live in cities and work in factories or offices.

Human Populations in the Temperate Zones

Three of the world's four most populated cities are found in the temperate zones.

POPULATIONS OF THE WORLD'S FOUR MOST POPULATED CITIES (2005)

CITY	POPULATION
TOKYO, JAPAN	33 million
NEW YORK, UNITED STATES	17.8 million
SÃO PAULO, BRAZIL*	17.7 million
SEOUL, SOUTH KOREA	17.5 million

* CITY OF THE TROPICS

In most countries of the temperate zones population growth is very small. In many European countries, such as Hungary, Italy, and Germany, the population growth rate is falling. These countries have more deaths than births, resulting in an ageing population. In the future these countries will have to support large numbers of elderly people.

Fact ZONE

Greenhouse gases produced by the United States contribute about 20 percent to global warming, followed by the whole of Europe, which contributes about 27 percent.

Farming and Factories

In many parts of the temperate zones people have had an enormous impact on the landscape and the wildlife. The land was cleared for farming hundreds of years ago. The rich soils were ideally suited to farming and large areas were used for cereal crops such as wheat, oats, and barley. The trees provided firewood or were used in ship-building and mining.

Countries of the temperate zones were the first to move from farming toward manufacturing. As railways and shipping developed these countries were able to sell their goods across the world. This shift from farming to industry has been the cause of most of the human-made greenhouse gases currently in the atmosphere.

Steel manufacturing is one example of an industry that produces greenhouse gases.

The impact of climate change on...

Food Production

Background

The weather plays a vital role in farming and food production. Temperature, sunshine, and rainfall affect choice of crops and their success. Some of the most productive agricultural areas are found in the temperate zones. Areas such as the North American prairies and parts of southwestern Australia produce large crops of wheat, which help to feed the world's growing population.

Climate change will affect food production in a number of ways. At certain temperatures, more carbon dioxide in the atmosphere will act as a fertilizer and boost the amounts of crops grown globally. Global warming may also change where crops can grow and produce extreme weather events, which damage crops.

Fact ZONE

The United Kingdom is currently on the edge of the European grape-growing region but with climate change more of the country should have suitable conditions for growing grapes.

Soy is an important food crop that could be affected by climate change.

Increased Food Production

In Europe increased temperature means that crops can be grown further north, in areas that were previously too cold. This climate shift could result in new crops such as sweet corn, sunflowers, and soy in the United Kingdom. Northern countries such as Finland are likely to benefit from increased food production from crops. In the **Southern Hemisphere** there will be a similar effect. However, if temperatures increase more than 37°F (3°C) farming production is likely to decrease.

Expected increases in temperature will result in faster crop development. In Eastern Europe harvest dates could be up to four weeks earlier in the future.

Crop Damage

An increase in extreme weather events such as drought, storms, and floods could decrease crop yields. Many people in developing countries who rely on farming for food, would be most affected by extreme weather conditions.

Increasing temperatures can increase the risk of plant diseases, weeds, and pests infesting crops.

Crop diseases, such as brown rust on this barley, could increase in temperate crops if global warming continues.

The impact of climate change on...

Human Health

Background

Many temperate countries have a high standard of living, with high average life spans and good medical care. Others, such as China, are still developing.

The birth rate is very low in many developed temperate countries, which means their future populations will have a higher percentage of older people.

Manufacturing in both developed and developing countries has created air pollution problems.

Fact ZONE

Global warming may mean that fewer elderly people die of cold during the winter.

Global warming is likely to increase severe and unusual weather events, air pollution, and the spread of disease. Elderly people are one of the groups most vulnerable to the resulting health problems.

The air in many of China's cities is already heavily polluted and some people wear pollution masks.

More Heat-Related Deaths

More frequent and severe heatwaves could increase heat-related illnesses and deaths. Elderly people are most likely to suffer from the heat when temperatures are greater than 91°F (33°C).

Poorer Lung Health

Warmer and more moist air due to climate change is likely to result in more air pollution in major cities and industrial areas. Smog forms when sunlight and warm air mix with air pollutants from industry and cars in still conditions. Smog will make breathing harder for people with breathing difficulties such as asthma.

Spreading Disease

Warmer and wetter conditions may increase the number of areas favorable to mosquitoes. Mosquitoes can carry deadly diseases such as malaria and dengue fever.

Flooding can damage water delivery systems, which can cut off water supplies or allow human waste from sewerage systems to mix with it. If this happens the risk of diarrhea and deadly diseases such as cholera becomes much higher.

Parts of southern and eastern Australia have suffered long periods of drought. This often results in poor quality water, which may need boiling before it is safe to drink.

Illnesses such as diarrhea dramatically increased when the Argentinian city of Santa Fe was flooded in 2003.

Forest Fires

Background

Forest fires occur on a regular basis in southeastern Australia, California, and the Mediterranean coast of France. These regions already experience hot, dry summers, and have a lot of grass and trees, which burn easily.

Climate change predictions indicate that the regions of Australia, California, and the southern coast of France are likely to experience more severe drought conditions in the future. These are likely to result in more frequent and more severe forest fires.

Fact ZONE

In 2003 Europe experienced heatwave conditions which contributed to a number of fires. The government of Portugal declared a state of national disaster after the worst forest fires in more than twenty years killed nine people and destroyed large areas of forest and many homes.

This forest fire swept across California in 2007.

More Forest Fires

Global warming is believed to contribute to an increase in forest fires in a number of ways:

- Drought, which will increase in some areas, produces ideal forest fire conditions. Dry grass and shrubs and dead leaves and twigs are good wildfire fuels.

- More carbon dioxide in the atmosphere, which trees use to grow, will mean more plant material available to burn in a fire.

- Higher temperatures speed up the loss of moisture from the soil, resulting in drier plant material, which burns very easily.

Drought produces dry plant material, ideal fuel for a fire.

CASE STUDY

Australian Fire and Drought

The 2002 drought in southeastern Australia was linked with an El Niño event, but its severity was the result of two climate change factors.

- Australia experienced its lowest average rainfall since 1910
- the temperature across Australia was 35°F (1.6°C) higher than the average temperature

With a predicted temperature increase of 1.8–10.8°F (1–6°C) by 2070 the outlook for future fire seasons is not good.

The impact of climate change on...

Winter Sports and Tourism

Background

Skiing and other winter sports are popular activities. Cold conditions in the mountains have encouraged businesses to spend a lot of money developing facilities to attract winter sports tourism.

Tourist accommodations, restaurants, entertainment venues, and miles of ski lifts attract a lot of money in winter sports tourism. Less snow because of higher temperatures produced by global warming may threaten this industry.

Fact ZONE

Using snow machines is expensive. Snow production needs special machinery, miles of pipes, and sufficient water supply.

Many ski resorts are topping up their snow cover using snow-making machines.

Less Snow

Higher temperatures in mountain regions have reduced the volume of snow and frequency of snowfalls. In the European Alps ski resorts located below 5,906 feet (1,800 meters) are threatened and may have to rely on their summer activities for their income.

Banks have stopped lending money to Swiss ski resorts located below 4,921 ft (1,500 m). They are worried they will never get their money back from ski resorts that will have to spend millions of dollars on snow-making equipment to stay in business.

CASE STUDY

Shorter Winter Sports Seasons in Aspen, Colorado

The impact of climate change is being felt in Aspen, Colorado, a popular winter sports destination in the United States. Winter in Aspen has started eighteen days later and ended ten days earlier over the last fifty years, shortening the ski season. In response to these changes, Aspen has drastically reduced its greenhouse gas emissions. Three-quarters of its electricity is now generated from wind power and **hydroelectricity**.

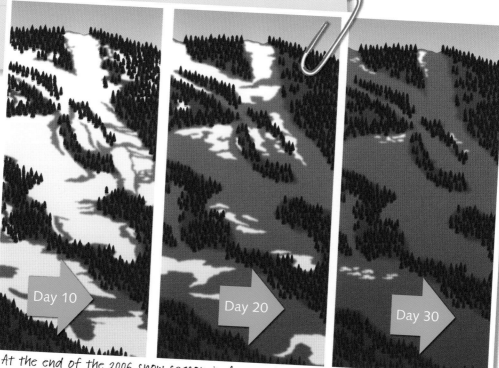

Day 10

Day 20

Day 30

At the end of the 2006 snow season in Aspen, the snow on Aspen Mountain took just thirty days to disappear.

Taking Action on Climate Change

Many parts of the temperate zones are vulnerable to global warming and climate change. The international community is working to understand and act on its impact.

Human activity is generally accepted as the main cause of global warming and climate change. Decreasing the amount of carbon dioxide and other greenhouse gases in the atmosphere is the best way to slow global warming.

Global Response

A total of 170 countries have signed the **Kyoto Protocol**. Industrialized, developed countries agreed to cut their combined greenhouse gas emissions to 5 percent below their 1990 level by 2012.

At the United Nations Climate Change Conference in Bali in 2007 delegates agreed to discuss a new climate change agreement to replace the Kyoto Protocol, which expires in 2012. These objectives were discussed further at the United Nations Framework Convention on Climate Change in Poznan, Poland, in December 2008. The purpose of the discussions was to set targets for future greenhouse gas reductions. Many scientists suggest that cuts of 60 percent are needed to avoid the worst consequences of global warming.

Fact ZONE

The United States, which has not signed the Kyoto Protocol, produces 20 percent of all greenhouse gases. Some people say the Kyoto Protocol will have little effect.

CASE STUDY

The Kyoto Protocol

The Kyoto Protocol is an agreement between certain countries that sets targets to reduce greenhouse gas emissions. It was negotiated in Kyoto, Japan, in 1997. Each country that has signed the Kyoto Protocol has agreed to its own particular target. The United States is the only developed country that hasn't signed the agreement. Countries such as China and India do not have to meet the emission targets because they have only recently begun to develop their industries. Other industrial countries have caused the current levels of greenhouse gases in the atmosphere to rise. The Kyoto Protocol will be replaced by a new climate change agreement in 2012.

European Union Response: Renewable Energy

The countries of the European Union, an official group of twenty-seven European nations, have agreed to reduce their greenhouse gas emissions by 20 percent and increase **renewable energy** sources to 20 percent by 2020.

Australian Response: Carbon Capture

The Australian population depends heavily on energy from coal-fired power stations, which are responsible for three-quarters of Australia's greenhouse gas emissions. The Australian government is funding the development of clean coal technology. This includes capturing carbon dioxide and experimenting with storing it underground or in the ocean.

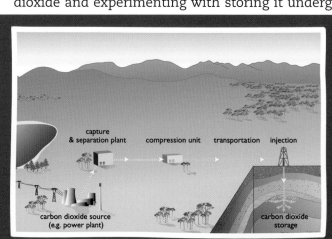

capture & separation plant   compression unit   transportation   injection

carbon dioxide source (e.g. power plant)

carbon dioxide storage

The greenhouse gas carbon dioxide can be captured and injected under the ground.

Community Response: Carbon Footprints

Most people in developed countries of the temperate zones have a large **carbon footprint**. Local governments around the world are encouraging people to adopt simple actions that can make a difference. These include:

- walking, cycling, or using public transportation instead of driving

- using energy-efficient electrical appliances and switching them off at the wall when not in use

- recycling

Many people in Copenhagen, Denmark, cycle to and from work.

The Future

Many countries in the temperate zones could be affected badly by future climate change. The temperate zones include countries that are some of the world's biggest greenhouse gas producers.

Heatwaves, floods, forest fires, and health problems are all possible results of further global warming. Habitat changes caused by increased temperatures mean that animals and plants must move or adjust to survive.

Setting an Example

Some countries in the temperate zones are setting an example by reducing their carbon footprints. They are doing this in ways such as using more renewable energy and developing carbon capture technology. Some people are using more public transportation, cycling, reducing their energy use, and recycling. These activities may prevent or lessen the impact of the worst predicted results of global warming.

go green and cut your carbon footprint

Reducing energy use at home is one way to lower your carbon footprint.

Glossary

alpine zone	area on a mountain just below the snow line, where plants such as bushes and mosses grow
atmosphere	the layer of gases that surrounds Earth
biodiversity	the wide variety of plants and animals living on Earth
carbon dioxide	a greenhouse gas produced by burning fossil fuels and clearing forests
carbon footprint	a measure of the carbon dioxide humans produce while doing their activities
climate change	changes in weather patterns caused by global warming
ecosystem	a group of living things and their habitat
El Niño	a change in wind and ocean currents in which the usual upwelling of cold water is blocked by warm surface water
equator	an imaginary line that circles Earth and lies exactly halfway between the North and South poles
extinction	the death of every member of a group of living things
fossil fuel	a fuel such as coal or oil made of fossilized remains of plants
glaciers	slow-moving frozen rivers of ice
global warming	an increase in the average surface temperature of Earth
greenhouse effect	the warming of Earth's surface due to trapping of heat by the atmosphere
greenhouse gas	a gas that helps trap the sun's heat in the atmosphere
habitat	the surroundings in which an animal or plant lives
hydroelectricity	electricity generated by the power of running water
Ice Age	a period when temperatures were lower and large areas of Earth were ice-covered
Kyoto Protocol	a special guideline that was created with the aim of reducing greenhouse gases
La Niña	an event in which winds blow westward across the Pacific Ocean, pushing warm surface water toward Australia
latitude	a measurement, in degrees, of the distance of a point from the equator
methane	a greenhouse gas produced by cattle and rotting plant material
migrate	to move from one place to another
nitrous oxide	a greenhouse gas produced from fertilizers
renewable energy	energy from virtually unlimited sources, such as the sun
retreating	moving backward
southern hemisphere	the half of Earth to the south of the equator
United Nations	a group of countries that have agreed to work together on matters such as peace, security, and cooperation

Index